First Facts®

Working
ANIMALS
OF THE WORLD

by Tammy Gagne

CAPSTONE PRESS
a capstone imprint

First Facts are published by Capstone Press,
1710 Roe Crest Drive, North Mankato, Minnesota 56003
www.capstonepub.com

Library of Congress Cataloging-in-Publication Data
Gagne, Tammy, author.
Working animals of the world / By Tammy Gagne.
pages cm.—(First facts. All about animals)
Summary: "Interesting facts, colorful photographs, and simple text introduce readers to the
world's hardest working animals"—Provided by publisher.
Audience: Ages 6-9.
Audience: K to grade 3.
Includes bibliographical references and index.
ISBN 978-1-4914-2052-2 (library binding)
ISBN 978-1-4914-2238-0 (paperback)
ISBN 978-1-4914-2258-8 (ebook pdf)
1. Animal behavior—Juvenile literature. 2. Beneficial insects—Juvenile literature. 3. Animal
ecology—Juvenile literature. I. Title.
QL751.5.G34 2015
591.6'3—dc23   2014032076

Editorial Credits
Kathryn Clay, editor; Bobbie Nuytten, designer; Jo Miller, media researcher;
Kathy McColley, production specialist

Photo Credits
Gamma-Rapho via Getty Images: Xavier ROSSI, 9; Getty Images: Photo Researchers/
Dr Merlin Tuttle/BCI, 13; Shutterstock: Africa Studio, 12, ajman, 11, Allocricetulus, 20,
Dimijana, 5, Dmitri Gomon, cover (top), 1, irin-k, 4 (left), Jody Ann, cover (middle), 15,
Johannes Dag Mayer, 14, Kletr, 4 (right), Margaret M Stewart, cover (bottom right), 7, Moize
nicolas, 19, Nick Stubbs, 17, PHOTO FUN, cover, Ratikova, 21, wormig, 22 (map)

Printed in China by Nordica.
0914/CA21401516
092014 008470NORDS15

Table of Contents

Ladybug

The work animals do naturally often helps humans. An animal's habits, waste, and food choices can be useful. Ladybugs can eat up to 50 aphids in a single day. Aphids are small bugs that destroy crops. By eating them, ladybugs help farmers keep the crops safe.

Fact: A ladybug eats more than 5,000 aphids during its lifetime.

Frog

Like people, frogs need water to survive. Instead of drinking water, frogs **absorb** it through their skin. They also soak up any chemicals in the water. Healthy frogs are a sign of safe water. If chemicals enter the water, frogs can become ill. When scientists see sick frogs, they know the water is unsafe.

Fact: Australia is home to more than 200 different frog **species**.

absorb—to soak up

species—a group of animals with similar features

7

Giant Pouched Rat

Trained giant pouched rats find forgotten **land mines** in Africa. Their strong sense of smell allows them to sniff out the buried bombs. Tiny harnesses keep the rats from running away. Since 2006 giant pouched rats have found more than 2,400 deadly mines.

land mine—a bomb buried underground

Fact: At 3 feet (1 meter) long, giant pouched rats are bigger than most house cats.

Vulture

Because vultures are **scavengers**, some people think they spread disease. But vultures actually help prevent diseases like **rabies** and **cholera**. They eat animals that died from illnesses before the diseases can spread to humans. Stomach juices kill germs that might harm the birds.

scavenger—an animal that feeds on animals that are already dead

rabies—a deadly disease that people and animals can get from the bite of an infected animal

cholera—a dangerous disease that causes severe sickness and diarrhea

Fact: Vultures often eat so much they are too heavy to fly. When this happens, they just throw up part of their meal.

Bat

Bats may look scary. But these winged **mammals** help the world in several ways. Gardeners use bat waste as a natural **fertilizer** for their plants. Bat saliva is used in medicine to keep blood flowing instead of clotting.

mammal—a warm-blooded animal that breathes air; mammals have hair or fur; female mammals feed milk to their young

fertilizer—a substance added to soil to make crops grow better

Fact: Like ladybugs and frogs, bats eat insects. They can eat up to 1,200 insects in one hour!

Beaver

Beavers are known for chewing trees and making **dams**. They destroy trees, but these habits are actually helpful. Beaver dams prevent **droughts** by keeping water in areas that would otherwise be dry. The dams also provide water to fight forest fires.

Fact: A beaver dam can measure 10 feet (3 meters) high and more than 165 feet (50 m) wide.

dam—a barrier built across a river or stream that holds water back

drought—a long period of weather with little or no rainfall

Dung Beetle

The **dung** beetle's disgusting diet keeps the world clean. This insect eats animal waste that could spread illnesses to humans. Dung beetles also bury animal waste. They use the buried waste as food or as a place to lay eggs. Some of the waste is filled with seeds that grow into new plants.

dung—solid waste from animals

Fact: Some dung beetles roll dung into balls. Females lay eggs inside the dung balls.

17

Shark

Sharks play an important role at the top of the **food chain**. They eat hundreds of old and sick fish. Removing these fish keeps diseases from spreading to people and other fish. Sharks also keep fish populations from growing too large.

food chain—a series of organisms in which each one in the series eats the one preceding it

Fact: Sharks are not as dangerous as people think. More than 350 shark species exist. But only about 30 species are dangerous to humans.

Bee

Bees do more than make honey. They carry **pollen** from one part of a plant to another. Moving the pollen helps plants grow. Bees help farmers produce about one-third of everything we eat. They also have an excellent sense of smell. People can train bees to find cancer, chemicals, and gunpowder.

pollen—a powder made by flowers to help them create new seeds

Range Map

animals' locations by continent:

North America:
Bat
Beaver
Bee
Dung Beetle
Frog
Ladybug
Vulture

South America:
Bat
Bee
Dung Beetle
Frog
Ladybug

Africa:
Bee
Dung Beetle
Frog
Giant Pouched Rat
Ladybug

Europe:
Bee
Dung Beetle
Frog
Ladybug

Asia:
Bee
Dung Beetle
Frog
Ladybug

Australia:
Bee
Dung Beetle
Frog
Ladybug

Oceans:
Sharks

Glossary

absorb—to soak up

cholera—a dangerous disease that causes severe sickness and diarrhea

dam—a barrier built across a river or stream that holds water back

drought—a long period of weather with little or no rainfall

dung—solid waste from animals

fertilizer—a substance added to soil to make crops grow better

food chain—a series of organisms in which each one in the series eats the one preceding it

land mine—a bomb buried under ground

mammal—a warm-blooded animal that breathes air; mammals have hair or fur; female mammals feed milk to their young

pollen—a powder made by flowers to help them create new seeds

rabies—a deadly disease that people and animals can get from the bite of an infected animal

scavenger—an animal that feeds on animals that are already dead

species—a group of animals with similar features

Critical Thinking Using the Common Core

1. Reread page 18 about how sharks keep fish populations from growing too large. What might happen if fish populations grew too large? (Integration of Knowledge and Ideas)

2. In what ways can animals prevent the spread of illness? (Key Ideas and Details)

Read More

Hernandez, Christopher. *Animal Superpowers.* New York: Scholastic, 2012.

Reyes, Gabrielle. *Odd Animal Helpers.* New York: Scholastic, 2011.

Townsend, John. *Amazing Animal Helpers.* Animal Superpowers. Chicago: Heinemann-Raintree, 2013.

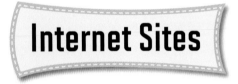

Internet Sites

FactHound offers a safe, fun way to find Internet sites related to this book. All of the sites on FactHound have been researched by our staff.

Here's all you do:
Visit *www.facthound.com*
Type in this code: 9781491420522

Check out projects, games and lots more at
www.capstonekids.com

Index